The
INSIDE
Room

INDOLENT BOOKS

ALSO BY LISA ANDREWS

Dear Liz

The
INSIDE
Room

POEMS

LISA ANDREWS

Published by Indolent Books,

an imprint of Indolent Arts Foundation, Inc.

www.indolentbooks.com

Brooklyn, New York

ISBN: 978-1-945023-15-6

For all the mothers we carry, and continue to imagine.
And for Tony, without whom—

CONTENTS

With her it was like
there was two places—
the inside room
and the outside room.

CARSON MCCULLERS
The Heart Is a Lonely Hunter

The
INSIDE
Room

Natural History

Petrified and fixed, I stare into the dark exhibit,
unable to distinguish between survival and extinction—
survive anything long enough and you too become extinct,
outlive a mother and you are no one's daughter.

We are past the Primates now, past
the reticulated python. Inside each globe
a daughter hangs—the damselfly's
inarticulate wings, the muscles of the stingless bee.
This is what it looks like to be held forever.

Persephone: A Postcard

In summer you slathered me. Robes, towels, lotion—
you wrapped me up. How foolish you made me
at the beach. You swam in a wide-brimmed hat.

Pale in August, you outwitted the sun.
More than Hades himself, you taught me to love
the companionable dark, fear the open,
unreachable sky.

The Swimming Lesson

I knew you best in water:
your crisp blue suit—that flowered skirt—
I remember how it opened
beneath my legs—the celery colored pool
with mysterious drains. I clung to you,
covered your pale blue body
with my own, as if it took two of us
to drown. You kicked, we struggled
to the deep end. Rootless, a ladder beckoned
in the meager sun. Hoses slumbered,
and nets for small caught things
hung from silver poles, hollow and remote.
You'd rescue anything that couldn't right itself:
beetles trapped on their backs, Daddy Longlegs
drunk on chlorine. Once, you nursed a spider
in the palm of your hand.

In the water you'd confess to anything, flatter me until
I could have loved you for it—the things you said,
little nets I took for affection, how you wished
you'd been loved, the way people talk,
I've been told, who haven't spoken
for years. You almost had me
believing I was your audience, the one
you flowered for. The place

was ours. Slowly I learned to subtract myself
from the listening air. Pleasure
had nothing to do with it. I practiced
the dead man's float, and you
kept on talking, alone
in that cold green water.

Afternoon Naps with My Mother

It's death not sex they remind me of.
As if we were two ghosts or plots, and sleep
the body we'd both been waiting for,
I'd lie down beside her each afternoon,
knowing it would happen.

This could be what drowning's like.
Who will be the first? That soft slippery body,
dolphinlike and smooth—that careless slip—
a sheath she wore so often I thought it was her skin.
I can barely remember what it was like

to take so many naps. I figured sleep
was just another way of leaving. In the morning we sit,
side by side on a green and endless lawn.
Insects unsettle themselves and drift,
slipping past the imaginary earth.

Determined to Become What I Loved

The girl who ate glass off the asphalt
in first grade during recess
was my idol. I admired the daring
to devour that much glass—
so green and freshly broken. I'd seen it,
wanted it myself—
all those cool and countless chips.
She vanished; I practiced.

I started small, worked my way up
from ice to glass: thimbles, marbles, smashed
figurines. I consoled myself:
sucked sea glass in slivers, savored
each new feat, each completed
experiment, the house growing
unaccountably thinner.

               That summer
I ate all the glass I could find,
swallowed light bulbs a hundred watts at a time,
I knew I'd found another habit
I couldn't share. A picky eater,
I saved the wires for last,
held them on my tongue. I wanted things
I couldn't touch—the China doll
trapped under glass on my mother's bureau. I liked

to take her dome off, cradle it in my hands,
as she gasped the air. I saw how love worked,
how the best was kept out of reach.
I hungered for fine crystal, earrings and teardrops on the chandelier,
those twelve Tiffany wine glasses
unwrapped by mother. I'd seen them arrive,
so invaluable and thin, it seemed impossible for them
to hold anything at all. I reached for the thinnest one,
bit a slender wafer off. Who could resist?

I decided to live

the way glass lives, to grow weightless as the swan
a glassblower makes. I saw it—
how it lengthened, grew wings. I wanted to swallow
the hot liquid zero of the swan's neck,
before it cooled, hardened, became
a swan's neck.

I am glass, I told whoever would listen,
filled myself with water, pretended
I was a vase, a flower. I lingered on light and air,
knowing I would crack. Like ice in winter,
I believed my body was an accident:
that once I had turned into glass—
I would be held flawless as light.

My Mother's Sweaters

Little drowned children in the sink,
so docile, so sweet. Their saintly
ineptitude, their incapacity for making
a single mistake: Who could imagine

their leaving the sink of their own accord,
buttoning their wet fronts, saying,
We won't be back, We're done with it—Their lives
shut in unlit drawers, the sudden and unasked for
closeness. The inexplicable tenderness
she offers them: the special soap, caress and rinse,

the way she lays them down to sleep
on newspapers covered with towels—
a crackling sound, if you come too close.

Their immutable sisterhood, summer after summer,
their only question: Will we be kept forever
in this house? I envy even this:
the decision is not in their hands.

Repetition

That time I told her I loved them both, said
I would have chosen them
out of all the parents in the world, *Come here*,
she said to my father, out of reach
and over my head, calling him, as if
she were the director, the only one who knew
exactly what we had to work with—where
the plot was headed, and how much time
we had to get there. Before the end
of this particular scene, the one in which
she asks me to repeat what I've said, asks me
to say it again, as if it were a confession,
something rare and difficult to obtain—and just before
she asks me to say it—once more, she will turn
to my father, now standing beside her,
hands at his sides. She will give him
these instructions: *Listen*, she will tell him,
You're never going to hear this again.

For My Sister (After Ovid)

When he cut my tongue out,
everything grew loud, then stopped—

even the birds. I thought
we were in it together: the storm's

temporary eye, the last,
harried cry. No more hearing

all the voices, clocks keeping track
of a different time. Imagine

the story of our lives
becoming our lives. We could go on

forever—our cries
unhinged from sentences and meaning.

No animal, nothing human or divine, not even
a small god inside—

nothing answers us, nothing
we can understand.

Sibling Rivalry

After the boys across the street
stormed the driveway—
ice balls in their pockets—
raw, boys' hands playing at war,
scarves flapping in the patriotic wind—
sheets and sheets of white—
salt in the dog's paws—
they hit him, too—ice-covered cars
stuck where they were, I couldn't lift
the garage door—couldn't see inside—
my parents sipping gin in icy glasses—a ritual
interrupted—Emergency Room
hyperbole of bandages and instructions—
When you wake up, the attending said,
don't open your eyes. Back in the living room—
my dog Bill at my side—I sat on the tweed couch
in my exaggerated splendor—the cocktail hour
finally restored. *Well at last you've got it*, my mother said,
the attention you've always wanted—her voice
lingering like dry ice. The next day—
the optometrist's office—bandages off—
then everything was milk—
shapes I couldn't see. I heard
the traffic's lurch and shriek, white
splitting into gray—the outline

and then the substance of things.
It barely missed, the doctor said,
the part that sees. My mother said nothing, as if
whatever happened to me had already happened—
long ago, and only to her.

Helen Burns

for M.H.

As a child I dreamed of being an orphan—
not *orphaned* but *orphan* from the start:
the noun alone. I wanted this the way
some people come to think of *home*
as a place from which to start.

In books, most orphans seemed
to have it pretty good, once they got past
the first two hundred pages of their lives,
there would arrive, as from some seed
planted long ago in the orphaned past—
the inevitable uncle, the blazing hearth,
all kinds of love and money (why suffer?).

Jane Eyre was nonetheless a disappointment
to the reader who loved Helen Burns and not
the idea of marriage—servitude so hard won—
call it *defeat*—it has to be confessed,
as in: *Reader, I married him.*

I failed to hear the good news, thought
it must be forgiveness that voice was after, considering
Mr. Rochester no match for Helen Burns:
her long blond hair, her stubborn cough,
her back against the English rain.

How We Made It Home

We skidded everywhere—the way my mother slid
across the kitchen floor, spilling
not one drop of her martini, missing
not one minute of the nine o'clock movie
she was always watching; the way my father drove,
repeatedly testing his breaks on the ice, until
he spilled us
in a snow-filled depression that Christmas
almost spent on a Texas highway,
all entrances and exits sealed, none of us prepared—
no salt trucks, no ploughs, only
State Troopers, *I'm sorry, you'll have to move*; the way
my father and I ran traffic lights—*No brakes*,
he made me scream, *We can't stop*; the way
high school nights I skidded—
eyes fixed on a glazed and cherished line, until
the boys I never slept with drove me home.

I Am Closest to You in Snow Like This

Nothing could stop that winter:
the endless snow, days without heat.
I watched it happen,

as if snow were my own self.
I counted the various fallings off:
the mail, the traffic, the mind—white matter

melting and freezing over and over again.
I swear I saw my father rush past in his tweed coat—
its anxious double hanging in our closet.

You can talk to the dead in snow like this.
Father, I wanted to tell you
how glad I was …

you had your body back. You never stopped
walking past like those shoes in the photograph
you showed me once: dark and empty, the right heel lifted.

I never imagined how much I'd love
that peaceful frozen motion.

My Mother's House

The first place I ever ate
hell's own fruit was in your house.
It's how I learned to love

that crimson taste, knuckled seeds like pearls
I'd suck and swallow. I loved
the patience it took.

And when I saw them in hell—
their puckered hides,
seeds in a dry and yellow house, I knew

it would be safe to eat. Once you offered me
this childhood fruit. *Little grenades*—
you called them this—

harmless on the sill. I opened them,
bloodied wrists—my first effort
at pleasing you. I've stopped

believing I'm the only child who's eaten hell's own fruit
to survive, who's learned inside her mother's house
what to eat and what to leave behind.

[Charlotte Brontë (1816–1855)]: Pair of Gloves

We outlast you.
In this glass box we lie
useless and thin as a widow's ring.
There are strands of your hair
we cannot reach. Slender,
you touched us. This thin skin
remembers your narrow wrists.
Loss is all we have. Around us
the curious remark, *Such thin gloves.*
We have lasted like the small clothes
of dead children—not loved
for themselves, but kept forever.
Where are your hands?
Let us feel once more
the palm of your hand. In the night,
winter comes. These days,
all staring and heat—
pointers and jabbers. Embarrassed
by this accidental fame, we dream
you will see us, break glass, rush
past guards, until
no one is dead and you
wear us,
leaving your house
for a long drive: the dark
Scotch firs, Verdopolis, Angria.
We have exaggerated nothing.

Turkish Coffee

There was so much smoke in that house.
I who grew up loving the theatrical
effect, mirrors and dry ice, never liked
that smoke, the way it kept me
out of rooms where my father sat
like the leader of a foreign country
famous for its bad weather, air
I couldn't breathe. In the kitchen
I'd make coffee—Turkish or Greek,
I don't remember. How it blazed,
almost boiled over like oil spurting up
from the earth. I'd pour it into his small
after-dinner cup, pour it just before
it boiled over. One night I tasted the grounds,
left like fine silt or gold in the bottom of a pan.
I never told anyone how much I liked
that bitter taste. My father drank it hot,
black, no sugar. I'd leave him to it,
that man I never outgrew, surrounded
in smoke. One day, I stopped making it,
just to feel what it would be like
to refuse even this.

Field Notes

Nights my father and I would walk the dog
one last time around the block
before sleep, and my father
would suddenly stop, and Bill the dog
would patiently pause, then sit, while my father stared
into the houses of strangers. The two of them
bore witness and observed—the tinny music,
the mouths of the brightly dressed
host and guest, opening and closing,
on the other side of the plate glass. *Draw your curtains,*
I wanted to warn them, while my father
took note of the neighborhood's
solitary readers, silent couples—and the distance
between them—countless families
sprawled on couches and chairs—the television's blue-gray light
spreading in the flickering dark.

And when I finally said it,
said the word, *Dad,* giving it
I don't know how many syllables, stretching out and back
in the embarrassed air, he turned and said,
How do you expect to learn anything,
if you never look? And I confess, that night I looked
from my bedroom window across the driveway
at the neighbors who lived behind us

without argument. I watched
their evening *draw to a close*:
the slow motion of Mrs. Powers'
bathrobe sleeves over the kitchen sink,
the end of a lit cigarette—Mr. Powers'
entrance, then exit—ice in his glass, the last light
switched off by the door.

Bulfinch & Grimm

In fairy tales there is spinning,
terrible wishes, and people
climb hair; ice splinters; the Match Girl
lies on the blameless street; and always
the dogs' eyes like saucers,
blind and hollow shapes; all the children
for whom death must come to resemble
an obtainable form of happiness;
glass slippers, mermaids, and rape
in the shape of a swan or some coins—
gold clatter and snow-white wings.
The stories are brutal, brief and fixed.
But somewhere a voice exists, if only
to tell the tale. Somewhere
a voice lies down and does not sleep—
here are its tracks —

They Wake Me to See It

This is the night—the burning
building, its flames. Crimson vermillion
purple and gold. *Look,* they said,
and I knew,
I'd never be able to tell
the difference between danger and beauty. I looked
to my father, the fire
in his eyes. I saw what it took
to get his attention, the way
fire ate the air. Anything
in that much of a hurry to get what it wants
already knows
there'll never be enough—
hunger like that.

I could hardly tell
the difference: their faces and mine,
orange and transfixed,
like the faces of shepherds or saints
in paintings. The source of light—
where does it come from? What was it,
what dark gift had they wanted me
to see. The closest we would ever get
to love, and no one there
to help us put it out.

Incinerator

In the apartment building
where no children were allowed,
it was my task to empty
the trash, to pour it nightly down
the incinerator's gullet. I'd approach
the back way—stairs
thick with gray paint and echoes
from landing to landing. You could hear
other doors unlatch, hinges
release. What lived
at the bottom of the throat, I couldn't say,
but I understood something insatiable
lurked below, something
they depended on me to feed. Who can say
what startled me more: the sudden
upthrust of ash from its mock throat,
that long chamber of unlit air, cold
with the ghost of no fire, or the times
I could hardly touch it—the door
to its shaft, that handle
burning my hand—my eyes
dazzled, lashes singed by the sparks
from inside, the world divided:
my father's rage, my mother's
refusal to be loved.

Gretel in the Forest

From the moment we entered
                the unfamiliar place in the forest
we knew we were meant to be eaten.

Even the trees spoke of it. We tongued the salt
                from each other's bodies,
knowing our parents wanted us

to starve. The father—nothing;
                the brother—
useless with crumbs in his pockets.

The one I could have loved, the one
                who watched me devour her home—
pane by pane—satisfaction almost

splitting my body in two—I pushed her in.
                I did this: barred the door,
listened at the hinge for hours

as she screamed my name—
                it sounded like regret, as if
she never meant the fire.

*

In this forest where branches fall like axes
                    I guard a single fire. Nights I pluck
a blistered lump of coal, take it

in my palm. Her embers feed on me, kiss
                    my flesh. I clasp the coal and chant the names
of all the children I have saved.

Like small towns, they talk, want to know
                    exactly what my hand is doing
tending a fire nothing can satisfy—

Sugar House

I am the indispensable witch,
the mother who gives them
sugar and pearls they will live on
the rest of their lives. Without me
there is no story. Who else has the patience
to watch Gretel devour
such sweet glass.
She likes it. While Hansel
rips tile from my roof,
I do nothing. No one comes here
who isn't already lost. Without me
they could have died
from hunger like mine. I forgive them.
Every time it happens, I come out
and build another house.

Gin Symphony

Night after night, my mother's orbit begins.
When the gin enters, her body goes
a little slack, then folds itself until
she's another form entirely.

On TV I see a man in white robes
who walks on burning coals. What
is the name for this? Of what
is he the disciple? He crosses
a bed of nails, steps into fire,
and nothing touches him. Is this

what my mother is doing—
stealing herself? The house
could be on fire, and she
wouldn't move. Nursing what's left
in her glass, she vanishes
and remains—the familiar
backwards rattle and forward rush,
bracelets and ice. Her lip's at the rim.

Night loosens its straps like a slip. Her body
goes under. My father's voice—nothing
touches her. Only somewhere inside,
I know she's there—reading deep and unreachable
into the night. *Let nothing harm her now.*

Winged Victory

Don't let that statue's headlessness fool you,
or her lack of arms. She's not that delicate.
Eight feet tall, without the head.

Just look at those wings, enormous and flexed,
arched back in the wind. Her body,
once fastened to a prow. All those pieces

shipped and reassembled at the top of the stairs.
Why is everyone walking past?—as if beauty
were something easy to ignore. Magnificent wings

like my mother's shoulders and arms,
those times she took me swimming
in the next-door neighbor's pool, her face

hidden from mine, the back of her head
inside the helmet of her scalloped bathing cap,
the kind with a strap beneath the chin—

such strange armor she wore, such strength
in her back and arms, wide as wings in the water,
carrying me to the deep end, where I would lift my arms

at the prow of her body, as if she were teaching me,
not how to swim, but how to let myself be saved.

Hunting Season

We are told to wear orange—
color alone could save us. A man at dinner explains
they kill only the males. I say nothing

about the small deer at twilight, the mother
grazing by his side, his sisters. . . .
I see them always at five, caught

in half-light and mist,
emissaries from another world
who must live in this one.

At the edge of the forest I hear them.
It is that quiet.
Mouths, lips, teeth. Grass

gripped by the roots, wet and rubbery
shrieks—strip after strip
rent from the earth. I love

their refusal to starve, their hunger
for this world—undiminished in a season of loss.

Window

Mother, you are all mind,
stoppered, gin soaked. Nights
your face hovers over mine,
keeps me from sleep.
You taught me: how to swim, not to eat
with my mouth open, not to speak
my mind. I flounder,
trapped in these words that circle
what I want to say, like water
spinning too quickly down a drain.
I am water, unreliable
like you. I remember everything I wasn't told:
about waves, for instance (I almost drowned);
about the body, its various mouths,
places you had no words for.

Now there is only silence,
the only child, ungrateful, the widow.
Oh, spider, how your web glistens,
sticky with tears, honey becoming glass.
The glass settles, runs
to the bottom. *Jump,* I think. *This is your chance.*
Mother yourself. Undaughter her now.

This is not easy. This is the ocean at night, the largest body—
what I want, what I believe I could almost—
if you would soften one moment,
Oh Mother, I would kiss you …

All that practice, my backstroke, no use—
I've hit the whitest layer.
I am motherless as air.

Persephone in Brooklyn

That was the summer everything exploded,
coke in sticky brown rivers, lamps that broke in our hands,
fuses that blew, a wedding gift, a crystal pitcher,
shattered, my husband lost his ring, and I
stopped dreaming, each morning a blank,
a void to fill with lists, pinned to a brown refrigerator.
I spent the season inside, read my mother's letters,
slept on sheets that never dried.

Unraveled in August, smothered at night,
I almost wanted
the coldest winter that came,
the cruel white air, the oven door.
I wanted to feel the summer
turn inside, to marry the earth,
now that I'd left my ring in the pine
drawer by the bed, dragged
the red metal chair
across the oak floor, determined to watch
those blue flames leap and grow
in that hollow place—
until I heard my mother's voice,
singing as she knitted me
a long wool scarf.

Sleeping Car

All night, the train, the dark—
flashes and sparks, fields glimmer,
and Pittsburgh—

all fire and breath in the night. My face
pressed up
against the thick, wide pane—

my mother's body slung over mine.
I feel all the space in me
accounted for, my body

a zero the night fills,
the wet stone smell, the green dark
mother, the wailing sound—

wheels, tracks, earth,
each hollow cry, and the night
listens.

Washing Dishes

Her tears sink salt into my whitest places.
I am thirsty all the time.
I drink and sweat through summer
nights, soak the pillow's damp
socket where my head lies
buried in that soft hollow. Mother
is sticky, takes the honey
out of my comb, brushes her long
hair into mine. You cannot tell us apart.

Subtraction (After Louise Glück)

Remember how you thought the world would open
like the small fists of wildflowers
in your hands. It was only natural,
the way you wanted to leave
what you had found; therefore,
you pared your body down,
as if for flight, as if
you wanted more than anything
to be first—*admit this*—in another world.

Sleeping Beauty

Last night when you asked what it was like
to sleep for a hundred years, I knew,
like any good thief, you only wanted

to know how much you had taken.
You with your two predictable hands,
how could you imagine

what doesn't look or taste like you? Each dream
like honey at the center of the hive—
there was no falling off, no greater sex than this.

Like some rough gardener who slices at the root
the things he sees and cannot name,
you parted this—it was myself you took.

A thousand shapes splinter and recede,
hunger quickens and repeats:
This is the world I wake to.

Limp and relaxed as ribbons,
my parents shift in their dozy thrones.
Most accidents, they say, happen close to home.

It could have been anyone's kiss.

This River I Keep Coming Back To

I do not know how the mind works,
but I know the way ice breathes in the night,
hisses like a trapped swan. I feel the ice

flex the muscle of its glassy lung, hear it
heave and shift. The nurse by the bed
drops her paperback, slips

into perfunctory prayer. I stare at the stiff
white space above her head.
You mean the world to me,

I say to no one in particular.
What is the source of this river, this storm
we have been tracking. The mind,

vagrant in some untenable sphere,
a blank against a blanker sky.
What circle have I too often traced in the dark.

Sudden Changes in the Weather

I didn't want to write about the dog,
my mother at the foot of the stairs,
the closet floor, boot smells and winter coats,
his delicate paws, packed with ice and salt,
how hard he was to get into the car,
how I slept in his circle on the floor,
felt the body's last kiss, that warmth.

Death is what happens at Easter
or August, when you're not looking.
I feel careless over losing what I love,
my father, a light put out by summer's end—
that August light (and I do not forget how you died).

That hot night I went to the corner store, and Mr. Paik,
who cleaned eels in the aisles, Mr. Paik,
whose wife would later be shot in the dry cleaning shop,
where it was supposed to be safer, he said,
Your father very, very gentleman.

I think death is a place or woman,
your mother at the top of the stairs,
she's calling your name.

August

I've never trusted anyone
who's given me flowers,
waxed and icy
in their tight-hipped rows—
my mother's friends
keeping her company that day
they made me choose
which ones for the altar, and which
for the fresh turned earth—
an ivory card for each
bouquet, a word
so out of place, I imagined my father
happy
he didn't have to choose for me.

Poem for My Father: Who Haunts Me Still

A cold house in winter, closets
stocked with gin, a woman's face
on every bottle, a woman I could easily mistake

for your mother—Your own life
leashed back, how you cursed
her plump memory, silk and sensible shoes,

helplessness and disdain. Night after night, you'd recite
the things she said—*It doesn't look well*, and,
He never earned a cent. The brother she favored

when you were young, the father
who killed himself, a man I always connect
with ocean liners and ink—the business he was in

all his life, a mistake. Years before I knew
what happened, I asked why you had stopped
writing stories. *No one*, you said,
can support a family on fiction.

I Visit My Father's Boarding School,
Try to Imagine the Walk He Took, and Fail

for E.G. and N.D.

I'll never know what it was like,
but I drove there once, and I want to tell you
I felt the cold loneliness of that place—

the early winter dark, ice-covered snow—endless
flat expanse—unfarmable farmland
interrupted by an asphalt strip.

Up ahead: no horizon line, waxy stars
hidden in a low-ceilinged sky—everything
hard, shiny, unyielding.

Nothing—no way to navigate, and where exactly
were you planning on going? Where else to go but back,
back to the starting point of *after, after, ever after.*

This poem, that walk—none of it
is going anywhere, only *after, after, after*
against the locked door of that night.

Who called the school? Who talked to you?
And did that person tell you then
exactly how your father died—

by his own hand?—What no one told me
all those nights at the dinner table. I only knew
the stories that you told, how your father

took you on a trip to *the Argentine,*
how you traveled on an ocean liner. I listened
until I could see that ship, undocking

from the dining room table, sailing past us
in the after dinner air. Even now,
it's that voyage I want to remember—

you and your father about to embark—
Can you see me on the shore? I am waving—
the two of you, side by side at the railing, slipping past.

The Silence of Houses

Everything died in that house: cats, dogs, plants.
Nothing grew. Underground, something
occasionally stirred. How else to explain

the basement floods. How lucky we were, each of us,
left alive. These days,
it isn't hate, or love I feel, but something

almost like gratitude
for the difficult gray, almost
windowless house, its black curtains and yellow door, its walls
covered with books, their familiar, foreign words.

At Night I Take Everything Off

and everything comes to me.
Like a postcard from the dead
my father's voice comes across—

a bough that bends
as it whispers, breaks,
Would you like an Eskimo pie?

I am a country that likes to be invaded.
Rivers rise; maps unfold; everything
breaks, rules, drives.

In dust and sleep I succumb,
I surrender. (This is my kind of sex.)
I am Egypt and this is the Nile.

There are gardens in the night
I alone can see. I roam
unlit corridors, encounter the dead.

My grandmother offers
an alligator pear, brushes her silver
hair, unclasps coral, unclips pearl.

Her hands turn to flowers, body to vine;
spider lilies cover her eyes.
I am summer and this is my fall.

I live through narrow escapes,
shipwrecks, train wrecks,
catastrophes that repeat.

Each time I sleep a sister dies.
She drowns; I wake, an only child.

Abduction

I liked it when he took me here.
My own flower with a hundred blooms, my own
chariot to hell.

My mother's a river now. Protected from the sun,
I swim in her silver-pillared caves. The dead I rule
are happy here. None of us suffer
in the dark.

How five o'clock would come, the way you closed
black curtains and said, *Thank God that's over*—
Sometimes I think you made me
just for this.

Chance of Light Snow after Midnight

Everything was taken that spring.
Unkempt and hourly checked,
even in sleep—

only alone in the shower.
Heaven is any tight place
you can stand.

I am made of this,
watery needles knit and stitch.
Ice in March, mud and no wine for Easter,

the minister's face so heavily greased,
I had plenty of time to remember why I'd stopped
going to church. We were few.

That boy's head bobbed from side to side,
uncertain and oblivious as any sacrifice,
like an unthreaded bobbin, his mind

all apples. It's Halloween in there,
still fall. He's only six months
behind the rest of us. Now

we are all thinking of apples, even
with all those flowers on the table, our altar.
His mother's small narrow

eyes shut tight
the whole time. You could see
sex didn't give her any more pleasure

than this. *What kind of perfume
do you use?* I wanted to ask,
disrupt the whole thing, my impulse

to take some pressure
off that boy, take his hand,
head for the snow

full of fallen fruit—deer
in trees like children
sent too early to bed.

The snow will cover us.
Body of Christ, honeyless night.

Photograph of a Dress

In the photograph you are holding me
over your lap, your arms
stretched out, as if to make

the greatest distance possible
between us, and still have it appear
as if you are holding me.

When I left that house I couldn't believe
the way people touched each other—
casually in passing, casually in speech—seemingly

touching all the time. I was astonished
at the lack of reserve, the ease with which
all these strangers touched.

The Anchoress

I am past all wanting now. In this grave house
my body winters. Night after sleepless night,
the wait for the light sustains me.
Through a grate in the wall I discover
how long the sun takes: the interminable gray,
the insufferable white, the beloved and eventual blue.
Do you know what it is like to wait?

Remember when you were a child and spring came,
the ice melted and snow withdrew,
and all was mud, the not-yet-grass and the pink
worms, and your mother let you go out without a hat,
and you realized what winter was for—
that all of winter had been just for this:
to walk out into spring, the early
warmth, the branches all bare expectancies
studded with green hints, all the traps sprung, and the earth—
I have seen this—how it wakes, rises like prayer.

Epilogue

Every myth's an obituary—people
turned into birds or trees.

Violence everywhere—.

Tell me, what is it I've become?

Exhibit

That day my mother told me,
You don't know anything
about me, I knew I couldn't touch
her either. Slippery with gin, she'd lie
on the tweed couch, a stone
goddess: headless, winged—
her shoulders chipped, an accident.

Too much of my mother is visible.
All those parts that made me have turned
inside out. Her straps hang, metal clasps
click and swivel, murmur, *Undo me,*
but somebody's already gone
and done it. I am extraneous.

Oh Mother, my first museum—
how you matter to me. If only
you were half as delicate
as you seem.

Doors, locks, keys,
you open and shut—a hinge
I must have lifted once, flown
out of your body, an exhibit—
a girl you couldn't take back.

Oh Mother, the lights
are out, the statues asleep,
the paintings hang.

On the D Train

The summer you died
I believed I saw you—
a pale, green cricket—
on the otherwise empty
subway car. It felt
as if I'd been granted
an extra wish, another chance
at forgiveness—the fairy tale
re-entered one last time—
not a curse, but a test
of a promise made
long ago. *When I thought
I could save you, I also thought
you wanted to be saved.*

Oxalis

I've seen them at dawn, turned inside out,
umbrellas in the wind—they catch
everything, refuse nothing.
What they do is what they are:
wings close, fans shut.
I think of all the seemingly delicate things that close—
plants, animals that recoil
from human touch, my mother's
heart, a garnet seed; the small
origami devices in grade school. Each numbered square
a child who dreams of folding, the way
cloth might fold itself, the way
her chest curved in, *We need to open that clavicle*;
the way, in certain countries,
everything closes in the afternoon sun. Exactly why
do they fold the hands of the dead—
Whose hands are these?—across the body.
The only thing left that looked like her, someone said,
were her hands. Folded like a napkin
at the end of some extravagant meal, for which
we are eternally grateful. What right have I
to look at prayer like this?

Rehearsal

After the chariot—its wheels
splitting earth—even after

I ate the seeds—

I was made to return—like a wheel,
dutiful, *decided*.

Every journey away from you
brought me closer.

Unsent Letter (Persephone to Her Mother)

September 23rd, first day of fall,
your stone is set. And I—
who never returned
your calls, never answered
your letters—am writing this—
stunned your sorrow appears
to have no end,
even when it is you who have left
this time for good.

Persephone in September

The myth has its own concerns, namely
the repetition of seasons:
the burial of seeds in the earth, the vaunted,
eventual harvest.

Whatever reappears is restored
to the mother—
Then there is spring. Also light.

It's how I thought the world was made
out of two people and the weather:
Disappoint a mother and you get winter.

                *

All my done wrongness, all my bad girlness,
          I thought all I ever had to do
          was leave that house. I didn't know
it would follow me—Also the myth

which has no interest in what happens
          outside the myth—if the mother dies,
          and the daughter doesn't
          become a mother: *No one will ever love you like this.*

Pilgrimage (Hudson's Christmas Windows)

for E.A.A., and for A.H.

Downtown to the department store,
the long trip by bus. First, the wait—
an act of faith—and then

the ride with so many stops—
an act of penitence, it seemed, until
at last we arrive: its towering,

massive sides. Revolving doors
sweep us in: bright cacophony and ballroom spin,
chandeliers like shooting stars, regal and anonymous—

elevator banks along an endless wall—
which door will open first?—
knock-kneed gates and levers inside—the operator

announcing our floor. Other children—
and whoever has brought them here—
am I part of an *us* or a *them?*—

mostly mothers—other caretakers,
grownups. We will never be that old.
We will never replace them.

Hats in our pockets and scarves in our hands—
gold posts and red velvet ropes—
a different kind of wait. The closer we get

to whatever it is we have come to see—
other people's voices—louder, then quiet—
gasp, chatter—hush: We enter

a maze. Where we are,
everything is dark, and what we see
is in the light—something cherished inside

each glass box, each exhibit
lit from within—and we
are permitted to look.

I think the world must be
a beautiful place. Each year—these windows,
scenes behind glass—my mother

taking me here. The time, the patience—
can I say, the *love* it took?—
for what else is love but time

freely given and spent. We enter
the winding dark, and the light
glows on us.

In the Space Museum

This, then, was what I wanted,
that downward rush through the angry dark
space littered with gray mothers,
deaf stars that candle
endless night,
flicker and dwindle. I burn.
Death has saved its roughest affection
for me. It will be like the sun.
I have traveled this far
to leave myself behind.

Children will come to the bodiless
exhibit and kneel
before my husk—
the one designed to protect—
even if they do not know how
to pray
        for their own safe landing.
My door will always be open.

ACKNOWLEDGMENTS

These poems originally appeared, sometimes in different versions, in the following publications:

Gargoyle: "The Swimming Lesson"
Mudfish: "Determined to Become What I Loved," "Sugar House," and "Turkish Coffee"
WV Magazine: "Chance of Light Snow after Midnight," "Gretel in the Forest," and "Hunting Season"

Many of the poems in this book began in Donna Masini's workshop at the Writer's Voice. Her class description spoke of igniting or reigniting a fire. Who could resist?

The poets and teachers to whom I owe my greatest thanks also include: Marie Howe, Sharon Olds, Galway Kinnell, Rita Gabis, and Jean Valentine. My thanks as well to all fellow poets and writers at the Writer's Voice, the 92nd Street Y, the Omega Institute, and the New York Open Center, as well as the Creative Writing Program in Poetry at NYU under the direction of Melissa Hammerle and with Russell Carmony's assistance. My great thanks, also, to the Vermont Studio Center where I had the good fortune to work with Lynn Emanuel and Jane Hirshfield.

I am indebted to poet Amy Holman for her close and careful reading of an earlier version of this manuscript; for her sharp eye, her unsparing focus and unwavering generosity.

All thanks to poet, founding publisher of Indolent Books, and now

Director of the Indolent Arts Foundation, Michael H. Broder: for his many gifts, including, but not limited to, his selfless, steadfast, and incomparable, if not close to incomprehensible, belief in what has become—all thanks to him—a book.

My thanks to everyone at Indolent Books, especially Samantha Pious for all her help in making this book possible—for her astonishing and seemingly endless capabilities. She just possibly may be two people. Whatever her secret is, I am the lucky recipient of her unstinting dedication to this book. My thanks as well to her assistant, Samara Rynecki, and to designer Adam Bohannon.

I would like to thank Frankie Drayus, Natalie Danford and Ellen Greenfield for their friendship and encouragement. My thanks especially to Sharon Kraus, Nicole Callihan, Lynn McGee, Carla Drysdale, and Jason Schneiderman. To Richard Peabody and *Gargoyle*; to Blue Mountain Center and the Virginia Center for the Creative Arts; and to the extraordinary Nancy Slonim Aronie, as well as Peggy Wallin-Hart and Philippa Anderson: my continuing thanks. My thanks as well, long overdue, to Ivy Frenkel Torres, and to the amazing Andrea Haring; to Sue Brennan, and all the many poets and friends who have guided me: my gratitude.

Finally, and, above all, thanks without end to my husband Tony Geiger.

NOTES

"Natural History," page 3.

This poem refers to the exhibit at the American Museum of Natural History, *Amber: Window to the Past*.

"Helen Burns," page 15.

This poem is for Marie Howe.

"I Am Closest to You in Snow Like This," page 17.

The photograph referred to in this poem is Dora Maar's *Pas Dans La Neige, or Shoes*.

"[Charlotte Brontë (1816 – 1855)]: Pair of Gloves," page 19.

A pair of Charlotte Brontë's gloves were on display as part of *The Art of the Brontës: Drawings and Manuscripts* at the Pierpont Morgan Library (now the Morgan Library & Museum). The title of this poem is taken directly from the exhibition label.

"Subtraction (After Louise Glück)," page 37.

This poem began as an assignment in Donna Masini's workshop at the Writer's Voice. We were to "rewrite" a poem we admired. However much this poem may or may not reflect, or live up to, the poem in response to which it began, it was inspired by Louise Glück's "The Deviation," the fourth section of her poem "Dedication to Hunger" from *Descending Figure* (Ecco Press, 1980).

"Sleeping Beauty," page 38.

This poem also began as an exercise in Donna Masini's workshop. Again, the poem may not bear great resemblance to, or live up to, the poem that inspired it: H.D.'s "Eurydice," as found in her *Selected Poems*, edited by Louis L. Martz (New Directions, 1988).

"I Visit My Father's Boarding School, Try to Imagine the Walk He Took, and Fail," page 43.

This poem was written following a trip taken with Natalie Danford and Ellen Greenfield to hear a lecture that happened to be at the boarding school my father had attended.

"Pilgrimage (Hudson's Christmas Windows)," page 61.

This poem is for my mother, and for Amy Holman, who encouraged me to include it here.

"In the Space Museum," page 63.

This poem began as an exercise in memory. In the summer of 1968 I visited a space museum in or near Moscow with my parents. My memory is of small capsule that appeared to me as burnt; that I remember as being severely damaged. What I saw may well have been the Vostok 1 capsule at the RKK Energiya museum—perhaps far more likely to have been on display than anything from the fatal Soyuz 1 mission.

ABOUT THE AUTHOR

LISA ANDREWS is the author of *Dear Liz* (Indolent Books, 2016). Her poems have appeared in *Gargoyle, Painted Bride Quarterly,* and *Zone 3*. After earning her B.A. from Hunter College, Lisa received an M.A. in English literature and an M.F.A. in poetry from New York University, where she taught in the Expository Writing Program and worked with poetry students at Goldwater Hospital and Bayview Correctional Facility. Chosen by Dael Orlandersmith as a recipient of a New Voice Poetry Award from the Writer's Voice of the West Side YMCA, she has had residencies at Blue Mountain Center, the Virginia Center for the Creative Arts, and the Vermont Studio Center. She has also studied acting at the Neighborhood Playhouse School of the Theatre. She lives in Brooklyn with her husband, artist Tony Geiger.

ABOUT INDOLENT BOOKS

INDOLENT BOOKS is a small poetry press founded in 2015 and operating in Brooklyn, N.Y. Indolent was founded as a home for poets of a certain age who have not published a first collection. But the mission of the press is broader than that: Ultimately, Indolent publishes books we care about. The main criteria are that the work be innovative, provocative, risky, and relevant. Indolent is queer flavored but inclusive and maintains a commitment to diversity among authors, artists, designers, developers, and other team members. Indolent Books is an imprint of Indolent Arts Foundation, Inc., a 501(c)(3) nonprofit charity founded in January 2017.

CPSIA information can be obtained
at www.ICGtesting.com
Printed in the USA
LVHW04s1740310518
579129LV00004B/852/P